Flinch by Ellie Rose McKee
www.ellierosemckee.com

Copyright © 2021 Ellie Rose McKee

All rights reserved.

This book or any portion thereof may not be reproduced or used in any manner whatsoever without the express written permission of the publisher except for the use of brief quotations in a book review.

ISBN: 978-1-8384323-2-4

Flinch

Poems

WWW.ELOWENPRESS.COM

Contents

1. Death Stages — Page 1
2. Cutting — Page 2
3. Cosmetic Cosmos — Page 3
4. Hornet — Page 4
5. The Soultree — Page 5
6. Childhood Home — Page 6
7. Stripes — Page 7
8. Spectre — Page 8
9. Tread — Page 9
10. The Giantess — Page 10
11. Wings — Page 12
12. Slabs — Page 13
13. Land Mammal — Page 14
14. Grief — Page 15
15. Delighted — Page 16
16. Shiver — Page 17
17. Shadow Puppets — Page 18
18. Déjà Vu — Page 19
19. Dark Days — Page 21
20. Life Lines — Page 22
21. Riptide — Page 23
22. Elowen — Page 25
23. The Moor — Page 26
24. Early Mourning — Page 27
25. The Sea Gaze — Page 28

Acknowledgement — Page 29

Flinch

Ellie Rose McKee

Death Stages
(Years 16 through 20)

The first coffin I carried
was my own—hopes
and dreams. White
for innocence; Heavy, for its loss.

The second coffin I carried for
too long—too deep inside me.
Ashes replacing the marrow
of my breast bone.

Mourning continued for years.
Resurrection never did come
easy. Grief had a slow

death, giving way to all
the wrong feelings, convincing
me that the numbness of before

was bliss.
Finally: new skin.
Always shedding, but warm
to the touch.

New life began with a scream.

Flinch

Cutting

I, the tree, several sapling rings

long ago hacked

                        from my centre.

Broken limbs evermore

reaching for the sun,

            slant.

You, the axe, recalling

nothing of the event.

                      Just another day's work.

Ellie Rose McKee

Cosmetic Cosmos
after 'Papilla Estelar' by Remedios Varo

Do you congratulate yourself in taking care?
In feeding light to keep alive
that which you have caged?

That thing which is a now no more
than a shadow of itself.

Don't you pity the stars?
Give thought to their sacrifice
in enabling such cruelty?

You can't force the sun to shine.

The moon reflects your transgressions.
Do not hide your face.

Flinch

Hornet

He was a hornet in a jar of wasps.
A mess of wings and legs
and stingers
swirled together.

Pickled in their own vinegar.
No honey here.

I was the child forced to hold glass
against reddened skin.
Fingers fumbling.

An accident.

How did the butterfly get caught?
How did the jar drop?
The glass get broken?

My fault. The *child's* fault.
Should have taken better care.

Should have learned my lesson.
Should have forgotten.
Shouldn't have dropped.
Shouldn't have held on.

No one looks back at the hornet.
No one sees him shake the incident off.
Fly into the sunny day, scot-free.

But me. Child me.
Butterfly me.
Broken glass girl.

Still, I flinch from buzzing.

Ellie Rose McKee

The Soultree

Her gnarled branches are a ribcage,
straining towards a moonlit sky.

Winter has been harsh upon the land,
stripping her flesh, but the Soultree
is a guardian, long established in her role.

Come cold, come wind, come lightning, or ice,
her ribs soon tighten, closing ranks to shield.

So long were the centuries, and so long
her weaving that, come spring,
the nest will survive: four unbroken eggs.

So safe are the beasts within,
they'll never see the light of day.

Childhood Home

Abandoned blood-coloured bricks
still house my fear
but now I'm at a new address.

The family tree wilts in the garden.
Wind whistles through its branches,
whispering: 'neglect, neglect, neglect.'

I no longer walk that overgrown path,

and the gate hangs loose on its hinges,
free to haunt itself.

Stripes
after the Fuco Ueda painting

Black and white stockings
skinned from the beast
pulled up bruised legs
to reddened knees.

By its stripes
she is heeled.

Sanctified by new skin.
Her flesh whitewashed with blood.

Spectre

You are the thing
that hangs behind:
                ever present.
                never welcome.

I've never written a poem
about you,
but your shadows are
                all over

my words.
in the background

you stalk my life;
stealing heat
and eating light.

Ellie Rose McKee

Tread

This house is old, the floorboards worn.
They creakily announce your being up
before the message has fully reached your brain.

It does something else to my brain.

My pulse jumps and my mind runs
off to things long gone.
Muscle memory in full force.

Footsteps on the stairs. The sound of judgement and
doom. The old house echoes, making light steps sound
like stomps. My mind plays tricks. I turn to the door,
expecting an angry parent with a ready word of reproach–
–

but you're there.

My heart stills. Arms open.
"Morning, love. Hear me coming?"
I smile, pass the tea I've had ready.

Press my lips to yours.

The stairs seem to sigh in relief.
I cast my eyes from the tread marks
of uncaring steps on my heart;

open it up to you,
my man of gentle step.

The Giantess
after the Leonora Carrington painting

They say size is directly proportionate to power.
She's not proportionate to anything.

                Sticking out like a sore thumb,
her fist the size of a gable wall,
the townsfolk fear her power.

(Her *supposed* power.)

She can do nothing,
yet they strike; try to knock her down.

A tower of folly—
foolishness stacked end to end—
stretches high, to the stars.

Nature turns their back,
pretends the Giantess is not their kin.

Skin scorched and ears ringing,
she wants to run. But where?
No land can hide her.

There are no hands to guide her.
Her mother shrinks in denial.
No. Not my baby.

Not a baby at all—
Adult-sized since youth,
she broke her back on the burden:

Ellie Rose McKee

all the power
weighing her down
rooting her feet in the dirt.

Blood seeping between her toes
as she stands, arrows in her side.
The ground rises up and

makes a home for the mountain.

Wings
after Cabinet of Souls (2016) by Laura Makabresku

She had such a beautiful affliction.
All of the townsfolk agreed.

Butterflies on the lungs were rare;
were the height of fashion;
were to be desired.

No matter that she couldn't breathe.

After her wood cocoon was fitted,
she had wings.

Ellie Rose McKee

Slabs

Sixteen slabs: grey, solid.
An ever-present part of my growing.
Watching over garden play like guards.
Silent, stacked at the edge.

My father bought them;
set them down, though
never into soil, never planted.

My brother decided to lift them.
We must have been short of a game.
I followed, tried to lift.
                        Failed.

Dropped.
Pain emptied my lungs in blood–red
screams, as toes became the filling
of a concrete sandwich.

My brother looked, followed my lead.
He screamed. My mum screamed—at me.
(Not him. Never him.)
I was told to shut up but still my bones yelled.

The slabs still stood to attention
the day we moved out.
I imagine them still on guard,
their edges speckled red, not grey.

Flinch

Land Mammal
after Brontosaurus Civitas by Jacek Yerka

Thousands of things came together
to build this ship,
sailing to a new land.

We make houses
from the bones of our ancestors—
give their bodies to the sea.

Carve out a new civilization
atop the surf.

Grief

       hangs in its web above her.

She watches its slow decent, the plotting legs, and recoils but cannot move.

He always used to deal with this. Always saved her. Always laughed, like it was no bother.

Without laughter, there is only fear. A helplessness.

It spindles lower, to almost touching. She'd scream, but who would hear?

Now just above her eyeline, she can see its mouth; the hairs on its body.

It watches, waits a moment, but they both know it is inevitable, now: the end.

It opens its pincers and bites. Swallows her whole.

Flinch

Delighted

She was Tinker Bell
Luminous in green
A beacon of light
welcoming everyone in

And you?

You couldn't resist
your itching fingers.
Yust had to snuff her
out.

Shiver

The moon is not your mother
She sees
but does not intercede

Night whispers these spiced lies
but you're most alone
when in his arms

Moon illuminates this scene;
is not unaccustomed to the injustice
but she does not step in

You are not her daughter

Shadow Puppets
after 'Temptation' by Mrs White

Death in a dress
reaches for life—
a shadow on the ultrasound.

The silence is deafening.
Bone fingers slipping
through holes in the ether.

She sags forward,
her strings cut.

Ellie Rose McKee

Déjà Vu

Once upon a time, a child turned
a page and found their future
mirrored – mired

in the black and white
of myth. Space like snow
between words
of Power, dripped

from ruby lips.

They are beauty
They are beast
Both and/or neither
varied by edition.

Repetition.
Reputation.

The magic mirror morphs
lies. Lives. Words riddled
with twisted tongues and double
images casting shadows over their kin.

A voice is found for the silenced—
not their own.
Legs are carved for the boy born
with a tail, trapped inland for too

many years.
Many times. Many men.
Not once. Not alone. Never an

Flinch

isolated

incident. Indecent recording
retroactively retold.
History no longer recounted
by just the victors.

Ellie Rose McKee

Dark Days

Darkness did not leave at dawn.
In dusk, all day, we sat
like clouds in a shroud above the ocean.

Waves, like ice, licked the shore—
promises of death on the tongue.
We flirted with it, then ran.

You, my shadow friend, return at night—
lead me back to those lapping tides
to dance an inch from death

once more.

Life Lines

The toe bone's connected to the...
root. Tied there, grounding.

The arteries, like jailers,
imprisoned him within the

mortal coil.

Death—a continuum
and him, in stasis; flesh

and bone as much a part
of the earth

he'll always be.

Ellie Rose McKee

Riptide

It's crazy how fast the tide turns.
How the sky darkens,
and a fun, family day at the beach
becomes isolation in an endless mass of grey—
saltwater in the lungs.
A pressure on the heart.

You cough and thrash—
fight again against the bonds you'd broken
long ago, and which you hadn't noticed
had slipped back on—

seaweed twisting around your ankle.
Your knee. Your thigh.
Subtle. Then suddenly tugging.
Dragging you down.
       Pulling you under.
              Churning your thoughts.

You won't do it.

With all your will, you push yourself.
Break the surface. Resist the urge to try and reach
the shore alone.
Knowing—*knowing*, in your rushing waters—that you need
the help you do not want.
You scream as best you can. Wave. Try and trust
that they're there—that they will see you.

And they do.

Flinch

Just as you become sure your last-ditch efforts were all for naught,
hands appear under your armpits and pull—
pull, pull—to the point of pain.
And then beyond.

You're being wrapped up in a towel.
Coughing up crustations for weeks, after, but you're on dry land.
You're on dry land. And the sea might
once again call to you. Might even one day claim you forever.

But, for now, you're safe.
You are alive, and you can breathe.

Ellie Rose McKee

Elowen

Still standing
after all the storms
and through many falls
of kings and countries;

her land switches hands
throughout the years
but her feet never move;

fed by blood
left on the battlefield;
she shrouds the bodies
in her own spendings,

season after season
and so stands,
still.

Flinch

The Moor

Barren land made of brown grass,
teeming with life beneath the surface.

You say the sun doesn't visit here,
but how else do we see the fog?

Ellie Rose McKee

Early Mourning

What do you do?

The alarm goes off, you shrug off sleep,
get up and nudge the body in the bed beside you.

He does not move; does not react.
His skin is cool beneath your fingers.

Your hand goes to your mouth on autopilot,
stifling a gasp. No. *No,* it couldn't be.
You watch for breath and think you see it,
but it's hard to tell. It's shallow, if there at all.
You watch some more. Call his name.

What do you do?
He's not moving; his body's rigid as a rock.
You sit down and run scenarios in your head;
imagine your life without him. Break your heart.
There! You're sure you saw it that time: a tiny breath.

An eternity passes in a minute as you stay still, still
watching, waiting for your life as you know it to end
or— the sound of a second gasp breaks the silence of the room,
interrupting your thought. He groans as he tries to unclench his
muscles. Your heart heaves. The world keeps on rolling.

There is air. There is pain, but there is life.
What can you do, but give thanks for a new day?

Flinch

The Sea Gaze
after Mary Oliver

I know what prayer is.

That summer was made by parents,
by three months of saving island one-pound notes,
a ferry, a broken-down car, and thumping
feet on a fire escape in the small hours
every night for a week.

Fifty pence pieces in the electric meter.

I made a break for the sea.
Lifted my face toward the horizon–
my full attention an offering.
My entire being wishing to exchange
my one precious life for that of a gull,
a sea horse, star fish, or anything

       free.

What else could I have done?
Tell me, didn't I feel
death looming
in every   inch
of my prepubescent skin?

How else was I to be saved?

Acknowledgements

Some of these poems were written during writing workshops with Jen Campbell, who also provided edits on this collection.

'Death Stages' was published by the Community Arts Partnership in their 2019 Poetry in Motion anthology, 'Find.'

'Cosmetic Cosmos' was published in 2019 by Poetry NI in FourXFour Literary Journal, Issue Twenty-Nine.

'The Soultree' was published in 2019 by Altered Reality Magazine.

'Shadow Puppets' was published by Black Bough Poetry in their 2021 anthology, 'Dark Confessions.'

'Dark Days' was published in 2020 in Re-Side Literary Journal, Issue Seven.

www.ingramcontent.com/pod-product-compliance
Lightning Source LLC
Chambersburg PA
CBHW021454080526
44588CB00009B/851